SEPT 2019

Project Learning Through American History

# ANALYZING SOURCES OF INFORMATION ABOUT THE
# U.S. CONSTITUTION

SARAH MACHAJEWSKI

PowerKiDS press

NEW YORK

Published in 2019 by The Rosen Publishing Group, Inc.
29 East 21st Street, New York, NY 10010

Copyright © 2019 by The Rosen Publishing Group, Inc.

All rights reserved. No part of this book may be reproduced in any form without permission in writing from the publisher, except by a reviewer.

Editor: Therese Shea
Book Design: Rachel Rising

Photo Credits: Cover Billion Photos/Shutterstock.com; Cover, pp. 1, 3, 4, 6, 8, 10, 12, 13, 14, 15, 16, 18, 20, 21, 22, 23, 24, 26, 28, 30, 31, 32 (background) Lyubov_Nazarova/Shutterstock.com; pp. 4, 10, 12, 20, 22 (insert) kontur-vid/Shutterstock.com; p. 5 Michael Ventura/Alamy Stock Photo; pp. 7, 23, (background) Reinhold Leitner/Shutterstock.com; p. 7 https://en.wikipedia.org/wiki/File:Constitution_of_the_United_States,_page_1.jpg; p. 8 Sylvie Bouchard/Shutterstock.com; p. 9 Nattakit.K/Shutterstock.com; p. 11 © iStockphoto.com/bonniej; p. 13 https://commons.wikimedia.org/wiki/File:George_Mason_portrait.jpg; p. 14 dotshock/Shutterstock.com;  p. 15 Firma V/Shutterstock.com; p. 17 Peter Unger/Lonely Planet Images/Getty Images; p. 19 Antonio Guillem/Shutterstock.com; p. 21 Fine Art/Corbis Historical/Getty Images; p. 23 Jack R Perry Photography/Shutterstock.com; p. 25 Justin Sullivan/Getty Images News/Getty Images; p. 27 Courtesy of the Library of Congress; p. 29 Rido/Shutterstock.com; p. 30 © iStockphoto.com/gradyreese.

Cataloging-in-Publication Data

Names: Machajewski, Sarah.
Title: Analyzing sources of information about the U.S. Constitution / Sarah Machajewski.
Description: New York : PowerKids Press, 2019. | Series: Project learning through American history | Includes index.
Identifiers: LCCN ISBN 9781538330524 (pbk.) | ISBN 9781538330517 (library bound) | ISBN 9781538330531 (6 pack)
Subjects: LCSH: United States. Constitution--Juvenile literature. | Constitutional history--United States--Juvenile literature. |  Constitutional law--United States--Juvenile literature.
Classification: LCC KF4541.M1455 2019 | DDC 342.7302--dc23

Manufactured in the United States of America

CPSIA Compliance Information: Batch #CS18PK: For further information contact Rosen Publishing, New York, New York at 1-800-237-9932.

# CONTENTS

An Important Document. . . . . . . . . . . . . . . . .4
The History of the Constitution . . . . . . . . . .6
Sources of Information . . . . . . . . . . . . . . . . .8
Using Primary Sources. . . . . . . . . . . . . . . . .10
Objections to the Constitution . . . . . . . . .12
Studying Secondary Sources . . . . . . . . . . .14
Think About It!. . . . . . . . . . . . . . . . . . . . . . .18
Analyzing the Constitution . . . . . . . . . . . .20
A Closer Look at Amendments . . . . . . . . .22
Be Aware of Bias . . . . . . . . . . . . . . . . . . . . .24
Examining Political Cartoons . . . . . . . . . .26
Put Your Skills to Use . . . . . . . . . . . . . . . .28
The Future of the Constitution . . . . . . . . .30
Glossary . . . . . . . . . . . . . . . . . . . . . . . . . . . .31
Index . . . . . . . . . . . . . . . . . . . . . . . . . . . . . . .32
Websites . . . . . . . . . . . . . . . . . . . . . . . . . . . .32

# AN IMPORTANT DOCUMENT

Do you have to follow rules at home? What about at school? Rules tell us how to behave, and they keep everyone safe and working toward a common goal. The United States has a set of rules that everyone must follow. It's called the U.S. Constitution. Written more than 200 years ago, the Constitution officially formed the U.S. government and gave it power to govern the new country.

The Constitution is one of the most important **documents** in United States history. Many historians, teachers, and students have studied it. Now it's your turn! As you're learning about the Constitution, make sure to ask questions. Maybe you will discover something new about this very old document.

### Founding Documents

*Along with the U.S Constitution, the Declaration of Independence and the Bill of Rights are two other important documents in American history. Written between 1776 and 1789, these three documents together are known as the Charters of Freedom. The documents give rights to citizens and establish a government. Each document is full of important history and plays a part in our society today.*

The Constitution is on display in the National Archives building in Washington, D.C.

# THE HISTORY OF THE CONSTITUTION

The Constitution was written about 10 years after the United States was founded. After the American Revolution, the young country started out with a system of laws called the Articles of Confederation. Under the articles, states held a lot of power and the federal government was weak. Government leaders came together to revise, or change, the Articles of Confederation. They ended up writing a whole new set of laws—the Constitution.

The beginning of the Constitution is called the preamble. Seven sections, called articles, describe the government and how it should be run. The Constitution calls for a system of checks and balances between the three branches of government. One of the articles makes the Constitution the most important law in the United States. Another article describes how changes can be made to the Constitution.

> The Constitution is written on parchment. Parchment is treated animal skin that's used for documents. Historically, important documents were written on parchment because it was known to be strong and long lasting.

We the People of the United States, in Order to form a more perfect Union, establish Justice, insure domestic Tranquility, provide for the common defence, promote the general Welfare, and secure the Blessings of Liberty to ourselves and our Posterity, do ordain and establish this Constitution for the United States of America.

Article. I.

Section. 1. All legislative Powers herein granted shall be vested in a Congress of the United States, which shall consist of a Senate and House of Representatives.

Section. 2. The House of Representatives shall be composed of Members chosen every second Year by the People of the several States, and the Electors in each State shall have the Qualifications requisite for Electors of the most numerous Branch of the State Legislature.

No Person shall be a Representative who shall not have attained to the Age of twenty five Years, and been seven Years a Citizen of the United States, and who shall not, when elected, be an Inhabitant of that State in which he shall be chosen.

Representatives and direct Taxes shall be apportioned among the several States which may be included within this Union, according to their respective Numbers, which shall be determined by adding to the whole Number of free Persons, including those bound to Service for a Term of Years, and excluding Indians not taxed, three fifths of all other Persons. The actual Enumeration shall be made within three Years after the first Meeting of the Congress of the United States, and within every subsequent Term of ten Years, in such Manner as they shall by Law direct. The Number of Representatives shall not exceed one for every thirty Thousand, but each State shall have at Least one Representative; and until such enumeration shall be made, the State of New Hampshire shall be entitled to chuse three, Massachusetts eight, Rhode Island and Providence Plantations one, Connecticut five, New York six, New Jersey four, Pennsylvania eight, Delaware one, Maryland six, Virginia ten, North Carolina five, South Carolina five, and Georgia three.

When vacancies happen in the Representation from any State, the Executive Authority thereof shall issue Writs of Election to fill such Vacancies.

The House of Representatives shall chuse their Speaker and other Officers; and shall have the sole Power of Impeachment.

Section. 3. The Senate of the United States shall be composed of two Senators from each State, chosen by the Legislature thereof for six Years; and each Senator shall have one Vote.

Immediately after they shall be assembled in Consequence of the first Election, they shall be divided as equally as may be into three Classes. The Seats of the Senators of the first Class shall be vacated at the Expiration of the second Year, of the second Class at the Expiration of the fourth Year, and of the third Class at the Expiration of the sixth Year, so that one third may be chosen every second Year; and if Vacancies happen by Resignation, or otherwise, during the Recess of the Legislature of any State, the Executive thereof may make temporary Appointments until the next Meeting of the Legislature, which shall then fill such Vacancies.

No Person shall be a Senator who shall not have attained to the Age of thirty Years, and been nine Years a Citizen of the United States, and who shall not, when elected, be an Inhabitant of that State for which he shall be chosen.

The Vice President of the United States shall be President of the Senate, but shall have no Vote, unless they be equally divided.

The Senate shall chuse their other Officers, and also a President pro tempore, in the Absence of the Vice President, or when he shall exercise the Office of President of the United States.

The Senate shall have the sole Power to try all Impeachments. When sitting for that Purpose, they shall be on Oath or Affirmation. When the President of the United States is tried, the Chief Justice shall preside: And no Person shall be convicted without the Concurrence of two thirds of the Members present.

Judgment in Cases of Impeachment shall not extend further than to removal from Office, and disqualification to hold and enjoy any Office of honor, Trust or Profit under the United States: but the Party convicted shall nevertheless be liable and subject to Indictment, Trial, Judgment and Punishment, according to Law.

Section. 4. The Times, Places and Manner of holding Elections for Senators and Representatives, shall be prescribed in each State by the Legislature thereof; but the Congress may at any time by Law make or alter such Regulations, except as to the Places of chusing Senators.

The Congress shall assemble at least once in every Year, and such Meeting shall be on the first Monday in December, unless they shall by Law appoint a different Day.

Section. 5. Each House shall be the Judge of the Elections, Returns and Qualifications of its own Members, and a Majority of each shall constitute a Quorum to do Business; but a smaller Number may adjourn from day to day, and may be authorized to compel the Attendance of absent Members, in such Manner, and under such Penalties as each House may provide.

Each House may determine the Rules of its Proceedings, punish its Members for disorderly Behaviour, and, with the Concurrence of two thirds, expel a Member.

Each House shall keep a Journal of its Proceedings, and from time to time publish the same, excepting such Parts as may in their Judgment require Secrecy; and the Yeas and Nays of the Members of either House on any question shall, at the Desire of one fifth of those Present, be entered on the Journal.

Neither House, during the Session of Congress, shall, without the Consent of the other, adjourn for more than three days, nor to any other Place than that in which the two Houses shall be sitting.

Section. 6. The Senators and Representatives shall receive a Compensation for their Services, to be ascertained by Law, and paid out of the Treasury of the United States. They shall in all Cases, except Treason, Felony and Breach of the Peace, be privileged from Arrest during their Attendance at the Session of their respective Houses, and in going to and returning from the same; and for any Speech or Debate in either House, they shall not be questioned in any other Place.

No Senator or Representative shall, during the Time for which he was elected, be appointed to any civil Office under the Authority of the United States, which shall have been created, or the Emoluments whereof shall have been encreased during such time; and no Person holding any Office under the United States, shall be a Member of either House during his Continuance in Office.

Section. 7. All Bills for raising Revenue shall originate in the House of Representatives; but the Senate may propose or concur with Amendments as on other Bills.

Every Bill which shall have passed the House of Representatives and the Senate, shall, before it become a Law, be presented to the President of the

# SOURCES OF INFORMATION

The Constitution is an old and important document. There's a lot of history behind it. For all that's written *in* the Constitution, there's been even more written *about* it. Documents, books, papers, journals, websites, movies, TV shows, radio programs—you can find information about the Constitution in all of these forms. These pieces of information are called sources.

A source is something that provides information on a particular subject. Sources help us learn and understand what we're studying. For example, you may see a picture of the Constitution. You also may borrow a whole book on the Constitution from your local library. Together, these sources help you understand what the Constitution looks like and what it means. Then, you can start discovering more about it.

The library is a great starting point for finding sources.

# USING PRIMARY SOURCES

Some projects will ask you to use primary sources. A primary source is a document or object that was created during the time you're studying. It's a **firsthand** account of history. In other words, someone who lived through that time created it.

When you're studying the time just after the American Revolution or the colonial period, the Constitution is a good example of a primary source. It's an original document that was written in the late 1700s. Its authors were people who lived through the birth of our nation and the formation of our government. It's original to its time.

When you study the Constitution, keep the following questions in mind: Who created it? What was happening during this time period? What's the purpose of the document, and how do you know?

### Searching for Sources

*Primary sources come in many forms. They can be writings from the time period, such as diaries, journal entries, and newspaper articles. They can also be other items such as photographs and paintings. Legal documents, scientific papers, video footage, and speeches are primary sources, too. All of these are primary sources because they provide a firsthand account of history.*

Look at this image of the Constitution. What do you notice about it? Where does your eye go first?

11

# OBJECTIONS TO THE CONSTITUTION

Primary sources give researchers greater **insight** into what was happening at the time the Constitution was created. Most importantly, primary sources give you **context**.

While the Constitution has been the law of the land since it was **ratified**, passing it wasn't easy. We know this by studying primary sources. When the Constitutional Convention presented early **versions** of the Constitution, some representatives, including George Mason of Virginia,

**From Mason's "Objections to the Constitution of Government Formed by the Convention," 1787:**
"There is no Declaration of Rights. . . . Nor are the People secured even in the Enjoyment of the Benefits of the common-Law. . . . These with their other great Powers . . . join'd with their being one compleat Branch of the Legislature, will destroy any Balance in the Government, and enable them to accomplish what **Usurpations** they please on the Rights & Liberties of the People."

George Mason, pictured above, was a respected politician and landowner during the Revolutionary era.

refused to sign it. They thought it gave too much power to the central government. Mason wrote his objections in a letter and sent it to important people, including George Washington. Look at Mason's words on page 12. Why does he object to the Constitution? What does his **opinion** on the rights and liberties of citizens say about the needs, wants, and principles of the new nation?

# STUDYING SECONDARY SOURCES

Secondary sources are another kind of resource you may use for projects. Secondary sources are different from primary sources in a very important way: they were created *after* the time period in question by someone who wasn't there. Secondary sources are a step removed from history.

Secondary sources may simply give information about primary sources. However, they can also offer **analysis** of primary sources and teach us new ways of thinking about these sources. Examples of secondary sources include books, textbooks, encyclopedias, journals, articles, and critical papers.

The books you read for school are considered secondary sources. However, they may contain primary sources, such as pictures, artwork, or political cartoons.

Now that you know the difference between primary and secondary sources, you can start using them. What clues can you look for to help you know if your resource is a primary or secondary source? Looking at the date is a great starting point!

There has been a lot of **scholarship** about the Constitution, which means there are many secondary sources about it. One of the easiest ways to find them is to go to your local library. The shelves are likely filled with books that examine the Constitution, explain it, and **interpret** its meaning.

Another place to explore is the National Archives. Part of the U.S. government, the National Archives preserves important historical documents and teaches the public about them. A section of its website, called "America's Founding Documents," has pages of information about the Constitution. When you visit the website, you can see pictures of the Constitution and learn what it is, why it's important, how it was made, and other fascinating facts. It's a great source of both primary and secondary sources.

> The National Archives is a government organization, so it can be considered a trustworthy source of information. Visit www.archives.gov/founding-docs to get started.

16

ARCHIVES OF THE UNITED STATES OF AMERICA

# THINK ABOUT IT!

It's not enough to simply read or look at a source. You have to analyze it, too. Analyzing means you examine something in detail, usually in order to explain or understand it. Keep the following questions in mind as you start to analyze sources, whether they're primary or secondary:

1. **What does your source look like? What clues does its appearance give you? For example, one look at the Constitution tells you it's probably pretty old.**

2. **What do you know about the creator? What was happening at the time it was created?**

3. **What is the tone of the document? What does that tell you about why someone created it?**

4. **What questions does this source answer? What questions does it create?**

Analyzing something requires you to think hard and pay close attention.

# ANALYZING THE CONSTITUTION

Take a look at the Constitution page on page 7. What do you notice first? You may recognize the famous opening line that begins with "We the people . . . ." These words are much larger than the rest of the document. What does that tell you?

### Six Big Ideas in the U.S. Constitution

The Constitution has six big ideas in its more than 4,000 words.

**Limited government:** The government is not all-powerful.

**Republicanism:** The people may vote for someone to represent them.

**Checks and balances:** Three branches keep one another's power in check.

**Federalism:** There is a strong central government.

**Separation of powers:** Each branch has specific, defined powers.

**Popular sovereignty:** The government is created and operates by the **consent** of the people.

Article II is just one short section of the Constitution.

The Constitution has seven articles that explain how the U.S. government works. Article II describes the executive branch. It says, "The executive Power shall be vested in a President of the United States of America. He shall hold his Office during the Term of four Years." The writers call for a president rather than a king. Given what you know about this time period, why is that important? Also, take note of how the writers call the president "He." What does that tell you about how the authors of the Constitution thought of women?

# A CLOSER LOOK AT AMENDMENTS

After the Constitution's articles are amendments. An amendment is an article added to the Constitution. Some states only ratified the Constitution on the condition that a list of rights would be added later. That's because the Constitution itself doesn't talk specifically about the rights and freedoms of the people. The first ten amendments were ratified in 1791, three years after the Constitution was ratified. These amendments are called the Bill of Rights.

The Bill of Rights contains some of our most valued

### Changing Times

*When the representatives at the Constitutional Convention drafted the Constitution, they wrote laws that reflected the country in the 18th century. Amendments allow the government to make key changes to the laws. This is important, because a country's needs change over time. Constitutional amendments have ended slavery, granted women the right to vote, and limited presidential terms to two. Think about an issue in the United States that is important to you today. What amendment would you add to the Constitution to fix that issue?*

"Congress shall make no law respecting an establishment of religion . . . or abridging the freedom of speech, or of the press; or the right of the people peaceably to assemble, and to petition the Government."
– First Amendment to the Constitution, 1791.

human rights. The First Amendment guarantees the following rights: freedom of speech, freedom of religion, freedom of the press, the right to gather peacefully, and the right to **petition** the government. Why were these freedoms so important for life in the new United States?

**23**

# BE AWARE OF BIAS

Some sources contain bias. Bias is a **prejudice** in favor of something or against something. Usually, bias is considered unfair.

Any source can be biased, so it's important to be on the lookout for it. It's important to question every source you come across. Questions you can ask to determine bias include: Is the author telling the whole story? Is the information correct? What is the author trying to get me to believe, and why?

Biased sources aren't credible, or trustworthy. A credible source should be an authority on the information, but it should also allow you to form your own opinion. It's important to use a wide range of sources so that you can get the full story and make up your own mind.

> The Constitution is central to American politics. It's widely written about and referred to by people with many differing opinions.

The
CONSTITUTION
of the United States
We the People
Article 1
and
The Declaration of Independence

# EXAMINING POLITICAL CARTOONS

Opinions can also be found in artwork, including political cartoons. A political cartoon is a cartoon that attempts to make a point about a political issue. You may have seen these cartoons online or in newspapers and magazines.

Artists created many political cartoons before, during, and after the American Revolution. These images are important primary sources because they give us clues about what people's opinions were at the time.

Take a look at the political cartoon on the next page, called *The Looking Glass for 1787*. It was published in Connecticut in 1787, the year before the Constitution was ratified. The cartoon shows two groups of men who are divided over the issues of taxes, debt, and money in Connecticut. A wagon symbolizing the state sinks between the two groups of men. Now look closely at the cartoon. What point do you think the artist was trying to make? How do you know?

What was the artist trying to say about the state of Connecticut during this time? What clues you in about his opinion?

# PUT YOUR SKILLS TO USE

Now that you know about primary sources and how to use them, how to analyze documents, and how to identify bias, it's time to put your skills to use. Choose something in the Constitution that you want to learn more about. It could be the 13th Amendment, which ended slavery. Maybe it's the 26th Amendment, which changed the voting age to 18.

Your first step is to pick a subject that interests you. Then, head to your library or start up your computer. Look for primary and secondary sources about this part of the Constitution. Find books that explain it. Do some research and see if there are news articles, journals, or political cartoons about the issue you're studying. Read and analyze them. What have you learned?

> Working in a group is a good way to learn more about a subject. You can learn a lot by sharing ideas with others!

29

# THE FUTURE OF THE CONSTITUTION

The Constitution is one of America's most important documents, and it continues to guide our lives as citizens today. Even though it was written long ago, our government still uses it to lead and the people rely on it to protect their rights as citizens. The people will continue to be affected by the Constitution as long as it remains the supreme law of the land.

As you know, the Constitution can change based on the needs of the people. Nobody knows what the next change will be. Is there anything you would change about the Constitution? Using what you know about the document and its history, how would you go about changing it? What would you do to convince lawmakers to make the change?

# GLOSSARY

**analysis:** Detailed examination of something.

**consent:** Permission for something to happen.

**context:** The conditions that form the setting for an event, statement, or idea.

**document:** A formal piece of writing.

**firsthand:** From the original source or personal experience.

**insight:** An understanding of a person or thing.

**interpret:** To explain the meaning of.

**opinion:** A view or judgment formed about something.

**petition:** To make a request.

**prejudice:** An unfair feeling of dislike for a person or group because of race or religious or political beliefs.

**ratify:** To formally approve.

**scholarship:** Academic study.

**usurpation:** The taking of something with force or without right.

**version:** A form of something that is different from the ones that came before it.

# INDEX

**A**
amendments, 22, 23
American Revolution, 6, 10, 26
articles, 6, 21, 22
Articles of Confederation, 6

**B**
bias, 24, 28
Bill of Rights, 4, 22, 23

**C**
Charters of Freedom, 4
checks and balances, 6, 20
Constitutional Convention, 12, 22

**D**
Declaraction of Indendence, 4

**E**
executive branch, 21

**F**
First Amendment, 23

**M**
Mason, George, 12, 13

**N**
National Archives, 5, 16

**P**
political cartoons, 15, 26, 27, 28
preamble, 6
president, 21
primary sources, 10, 12, 14, 15, 18, 26, 28

**S**
secondary sources, 14, 15, 16, 18, 28

**T**
13th Amendment, 28
26th Amendment, 28

**U**
United States, 4, 6, 21, 22, 23

**V**
Virginia, 12

**W**
Washington, D.C., 5
Washington, George, 13

# WEBSITES

Due to the changing nature of Internet links, PowerKids Press has developed an online list of websites related to the subject of this book. This site is updated regularly. Please use this link to access the list: www.powerkidslinks.com/pltam/ana